FOOTBALL FOCUS

WORLD CUP FOOTBALL

Clive Gifford

WAYLAND

First published in 2014 by Wayland

Copyright © Wayland 2014

Wayland
338 Euston Road
London NW1 3BH

Wayland Australia
Level 17/207, Kent Street
Sydney, NSW 2000

Editor: Nicola Edwards
Designer: Basement 68

A catalogue record for this book is available
from the British Library.

Dewey categorisation: 796

ISBN 978 0 7502 8287 1

Printed in China

10 9 8 7 6 5 4 3 2 1

Wayland is a division of Hachette Children's Books,
an Hachette UK company.

www.hachette.co.uk

The author and publisher would like to thank the
following for allowing their images to be used in
this book: Cover: all Shutterstock; title page: Javier
Soriano/AFP/Getty Images p2 Bill Kret/Shutterstock.
com; p4 fstockfoto / Shutterstock.com; p5 (t) istock ©
jcamilobernal, (b) AFP/Getty Images; p6 Popperfoto/
Getty Images; p7; Popperfoto/Getty Images; p8 (main)
Shutterstock © Celso Pupo, (inset) Globo via Getty
Images; p9 FIFA via Getty Images; p10 mooinblack /
Shutterstock.com; p11 Laszlo Szirtesi / Shutterstock.
com; p12 (l) fstockfoto / Shutterstock.com, (r) Bill Kret/
Shutterstock.com; p13 LatinContent/Getty Images;
p14 FIFA via Getty Images; p15 Getty Images; p16
Getty Images; p17 AFP/Getty Images; p18 Bongarts/
Getty Images; p19 AFP/Getty Images; p20 AFP/Getty
Images; p21 Roberto Schmidt/AFP/Getty Images; p22
Getty Images; p23 Javier Soriano/AFP/Getty Images; p24
Getty Images; p25 Getty Images for adidas; p26 Christof
Stache/AFP/Getty Images; p27 AFP/Getty Images; p28
Time & Life Pictures/Getty Images; p29 Staff/AFP/Getty
Images; p30 Shutterstock © Maxisport

CONTENTS

Football's biggest competition

Every four years, the cream of the world's greatest footballers and national teams come together in a contest to be crowned the sport's world champions. The tournament they take part in is the FIFA World Cup.

Global game

FIFA is short for *Fédération Internationale de Football Association*. Based in Zurich, Switzerland, it is the organisation that runs world football and organises the World Cup. The tournament has grown from its small beginnings to become the biggest single sports event in the world. More than a billion people watch games on TV or via the Internet, and stadia are packed with spectators who get to see the action live.

Over 3.1 million fans saw live games at the 2010 World Cup and 619.7 million people watched at least 20 minutes of the 2010 World Cup Final between Spain and the Netherlands. For top professional footballers, even those that have won other competitions with their club or country, it is the ultimate goal to become a World Cup winner.

Brazil play North Korea at the 2010 World Cup. The tournament attracts teams from all over the world.

Trophy talk

The winners of early World Cups were awarded the Jules Rimet trophy, named after the French football official who had first suggested the competition. Rimet would go on to become FIFA's longest-serving president (1921-54). The trophy was kept by Brazil in 1970 after they had won the World Cup three times, and a new trophy made for the 1974 tournament. The winning design from 53 entrants was by Italian artist Silvio Gazzaniga and features figures holding Earth above them. Cast in 18 carat gold, the trophy stays with FIFA but World Cup winning countries are given a replica to keep.

The FIFA World Cup trophy is 36.5cm tall, weighs 6.175kg and is the most sought-after prize in world football.

ON THE BALL

The original World Cup trophy was stolen months before the 1966 World Cup. A panic ensued until a collie dog called Pickles discovered it under a hedge in south London.

Argentina's Lionel Messi (right) prepares to shoot during one of the qualifying matches that secured Argentina a place at the 2014 World Cup.

" Winning the World Cup is what is missing. The truth is, yes, I would swap a Ballon D'Or for the World Cup...Nothing compares with being world champion."

Lionel Messi
winner of the Ballon D'Or
(or 'Golden Ball') for the
World's Best Player

World Cup beginnings

The first World Cup was held in 1930. The then Olympic football champions, Uruguay, were chosen as the country that would host the tournament. Only 13 countries decided to attend the competition, all either from Europe or the Americas.

Route to success

Three of the four European teams (France, Belgium and Romania) sailed across the Atlantic in the SS *Conte Verde* along with Jules Rimet and the newly-minted World Cup trophy. They picked up the Brazilian team along the way and arrived in Uruguay to join teams from the USA and Mexico, Yugoslavia and seven South American nations. Two of these – Uruguay and Argentina – contested the final after both thrashing their semi-final opponents 6-1. Uruguay won 4-2 in front of 93,000 spectators to become the first ever World Cup winners.

Uruguay's captain Jose Nasazzi (left) shakes hands with Argentinean skipper, Manuel Ferreira before the start of the 1930 World Cup Final. Uruguay's fourth goal was scored by Héctor Castro, who had lost his lower right arm in an accident as a teenager.

6

The 1934 and 1938 World Cups

Unimpressed at the lack of entrants from Europe at their tournament, Uruguay chose to snub the next World Cup, which was held in Italy in 1934. Thirty-two teams applied to take part in the 16-team competition. This meant that for the first time qualifying matches had to played, during which Egypt became the first African team to reach a World Cup. The tournament was again won by the home team, who beat Czechoslovakia in the final. Italy managed to repeat their triumph at the 1938 World Cup, which was held in France.

"

We came in at half-time in that game 2-1 ahead…We couldn't hold on to our lead. I can still remember the euphoria that reigned in the stands. It was a blow I've spent my entire life trying to get over.

Francisco Varallo
Argentinean attacker in the 1930 World Cup Final

"

A poster promoting the 1938 World Cup in France. During the tournament's 18 games, which were held in nine different French cities, 84 goals were scored.

7

Hosting a World Cup

Long before a World Cup is held, its first competitive act is the battle between nations for the right to host the tournament. The winning country or countries are announced many years before the tournament. They have a major task on their hands to get everything ready in time for the first kick-off.

Bidding to win

Most World Cups attract a number of bids. Competing countries have to convince the FIFA executive committee that theirs is the best, and tension mounts before the announcement is made. Unusually, Brazil's was the only bid for the 2014 World Cup, making the country the fifth nation to host the competition twice (along with Germany, France, Italy and Mexico). Only the 2002 World Cup has been held jointly by two countries, Japan and South Korea. It was also the first World Cup to be held in Asia. In 2010, the hosts of the 2018 (Russia) and 2022 (Qatar) World Cups were announced.

Pelé (right) and Dunga, Brazil coach in 2009, hold up replicas of the two World Cup trophies to celebrate the tournament coming to Rio de Janeiro, Brazil in 2014. Many promotional events are held in the years before a World Cup.

Getting things right

The real work and financial costs begin as soon as the winning bid is announced. A host nation has to build new stadia and refurbish old ones to bring them up to standard. But that is only part of the story. The country has to be ready for the arrival of several million football fans, 32 teams and their support staff and much of the world's sports media – over 15,000 of them at the 2010 World Cup. Transport links, training facilities, major security and extra events for fans all have to be created, and more than three million tickets sold.

> *It's a big responsibility for Brazil because we will host the greatest events in sports history. Brazil must prove that, as a country, we are not only good on the field, but off the field as well.*
>
> **Brazilian World Cup legend Pelé**
> speaking about hosting
> the 2014 World Cup

The famous Maracana stadium in Rio de Janeiro underwent major building works to be ready for the 2014 World Cup as host venue for group games and the Final. The first official match at the revamped stadium was a friendly between Brazil and England in 2013.

Ever since 1966, each tournament has one or more cute and cuddly mascots as the face of the tournament. The 2014 World Cup mascot was an armadillo called Fuleco.

Qualifying for the tournament

With around 200 national sides wanting to take part in a World Cup but only 32 places available, qualifying competitions have to be held. These matches can be tense, nail-biting affairs, for players and fans alike.

Continental competitions

Teams qualify by playing a series of matches against other sides within their continent. More than 800 qualifying matches are played in total. Each continent has a set number of places at the World Cup. Currently, Europe has the lion's share with 13 places. A place is also reserved for the hosts of the tournament.

In addition one team each from South America, CONCACAF (which includes north and central America and the Caribbean), Asia and Oceania take part in play-off matches. The two play-off winners also make it to the World Cup.

Carl Valeri of Australia is surrounded by Thailand defenders as the two teams compete in a qualifying game for a place at the 2014 World Cup in Brazil.

Winners and losers

Only Brazil have taken part in every single World Cup. Many other teams, including well-regarded sides, have to endure heartbreak and failure to qualify. This includes England (who have failed to qualify three times) Spain (four times), France (five times) and Portugal (13 times). Shock results occur in every qualifying campaign, such as Armenia's 4-0 defeat of Denmark and Honduras beating USA 2-1, both in 2013. But little can compete with the enormous victory Australia notched up in 2001 against American Samoa, a world record score in international football of 31-0, with striker Archie Thomson scoring 13 times.

> *As a kid growing up in the back streets of Dublin I used to pretend I was playing in the World Cup with my mates out on the streets, and now I will be doing it for real.*
>
> **Robbie Keane**
> on the Republic of Ireland qualifying for the 2006 World Cup.

Robin van Persie turns to avoid a challenge from Hungary's Roland Juhász during the 4-1 away victory for the Netherlands in the 2014 qualifying campaign. Despite reaching the World Cup Final match three times, the Dutch have also failed to qualify for seven tournaments.

World Cup fans

Fans flock to each World Cup competition to enjoy the big tournament atmosphere, support their team, and watch big games. The scramble for tickets begins many months before the tournament starts.

National pride

For many football fans, going to a World Cup is the ultimate supporter challenge. Tickets can be hard to obtain and travel and accommodation expensive. Yet this does not deter hundreds of thousands from travelling to the host nation and proudly wearing their national team colours. The atmosphere is one of excitement with different countries' fans mixing cheerfully, but security is on hand just in case there is any trouble. In the past, some games weren't well attended. Only 300 turned up to watch Romania v Peru in 1930, for example. Today, almost all 64 games of each World Cup are sell-outs.

> *The atmosphere in South Africa was amazing – having the chance to watch some of the biggest football games in the world in such a beautiful country is something I won't ever forget.*

Adri Pols
Dutch fan at the 2010 World Cup

Dutch fans turn the city of Leipzig orange during the 2006 World Cup, which was held in Germany.

A South African supporter blows a vuvuzela during his side's 2010 World Cup match against Mexico. These extremely noisy plastic horns were played in their thousands by fans at the 2010 World Cup.

Fan Fests

Many fans travel to host nations either without any match tickets or wanting to see games other than those for which they have tickets. In recent World Cups, host nations have created fan zones known as Fan Fests to fulfil the enormous demand to watch live TV broadcasts of games in big match atmosphere. These large areas hold thousands of fans and are equipped with enormous TV screens showing the action as well as other entertainments including music, competitions, circus performers and celebrity appearances by famous football legends. At the 2010 World Cup, over six million people attended Fan Fests in South Africa.

Numbers Game

More than 3 million fans watched live games at the 2006 and 2010 World Cup, but the biggest total World Cup attendance was in the USA in 1994. There, 3,587,538 fans watched the 52 games live, an average of 68,991 per game.

FIFA Fan Fests are also held outside the country hosting the World Cup. This giant screen was set up in Rio de Janeiro for Brazilian fans to watch the 2010 World Cup, held in South Africa.

World Cup coaches

A manager or head coach of a national team has the huge responsibility of selecting players and tactics to guarantee that the team reaches a World Cup and then performs well at it.

A coach's duties

Before a World Cup, each national coach chooses 23 players to take as his squad. That may sound a lot, but most coaches would take more if they could to guard against injuries and to give them a range of players for different styles of play. A coach's choices can provoke outrage in the media, particularly if popular players are left out. Such was the fate of Samir Nasri of France, Francesco Totti of Italy and Brazil's Adriano and Ronaldinho in 2010.

From this squad of 23 players, each coach selects and prepares his starting eleven for each game, tailoring tactics to overcome that match's opponents. As a tournament progresses, a coach may have to alter his plans as players perform above or below expectations and injuries mount.

Brazil's coach for the 2014 World Cup, Luiz Felipe Scolari, instructs his players during a training session.

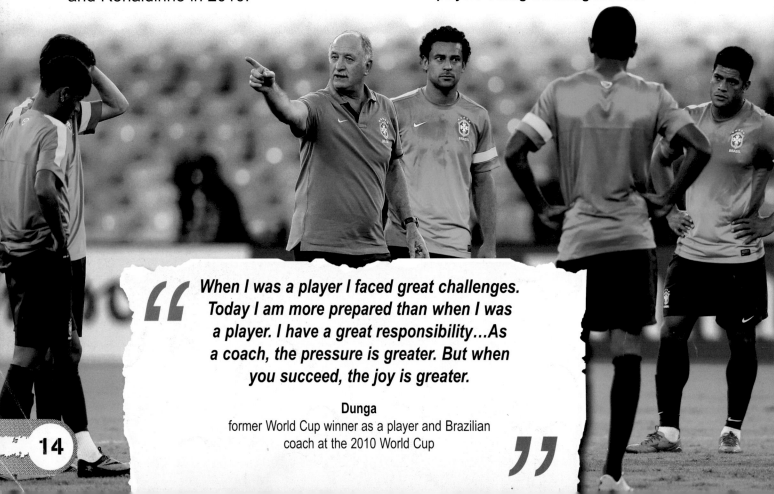

When I was a player I faced great challenges. Today I am more prepared than when I was a player. I have a great responsibility...As a coach, the pressure is greater. But when you succeed, the joy is greater.

Dunga
former World Cup winner as a player and Brazilian coach at the 2010 World Cup

ON THE BALL

Brazil coach Ademar Pimenta rested his star player, Leonidas, for the 1938 semi-final against Italy. It proved a disastrous decision as Italy knocked out Brazil, 2-1.

Coaching records

No foreign coach of a team has ever won the World Cup, but that hasn't stopped countries picking a coach from abroad to guide their national side. Carlos Alberto Parreira has appeared as a coach at six different World Cups with five different teams: Kuwait, UAE, Brazil, Saudi Arabia and, at the 2010 World Cup, South Africa. He won the World Cup once with Brazil in 1994. Only one coach has won the World Cup twice – Italy's Vittorio Pozzo in 1934 and 1938, but two have won it first as a player and then as a coach – Brazilian Mario Zagallo in 1958 and 1970 and Franz Beckenbauer in 1974 and 1990.

Vicente del Bosque (left) gestures at his Spanish players while the opposition coach, Bert van Marwijk of the Netherlands, stands on the touchline nearby during the 2010 World Cup Final. Spain won the match 1-0 after extra time.

Attack and defence

Every football match is a contest between each team's attacking play and the opposing team's defence. Teams rarely do well at a World Cup without a strong defence and commanding goalkeeper, but also need midfielders and strikers with a serious eye for goal.

Thrills and spills

Teams play in different styles depending on the types of player they have and the opponents and situation they face. Early group games at a World Cup, for example, are often tight, cagey affairs with defences dominating as neither side wants to slip up and lose. Sometimes, one of the tournament favourites can be shocked by opponents who prove outstanding in defence, such as Spain's surprise 1-0 loss to Switzerland in their first 2010 World Cup game. On other occasions, a mismatch occurs such as Portugal's 7-0 thrashing of North Korea in 2010 or the all-time record scoreline at a World Cup - Hungary 10, El Salvador 1 in 1982.

Spain's David Villa drives the ball past Eduardo, the Portugal keeper, during the 2010 World Cup to score one of his five goals in the tournament.

Scoring and stopping goals

Teams may rely on their attackers for most of their goals, but crucial scores can also be made by defenders and midfielders. One of the three leading scorers at the 2010 World Cup was a midfielder, Germany's Thomas Müller, and Italy's sole goal in the 2006 Final was scored by central defender, Marco Materazzi. Defenders work closely with the goalkeeper to repel opposition attacks and aim to keep a clean sheet. Three of the last four World Cup winning goalkeepers (Fabien Barthez in 1998, Gianluigi Buffon in 2006 and Iker Casillas in 2010) only conceded two goals in their seven games.

Paraguay keeper Justo Villar dives for the ball at the feet of Spain's Cesc Fàbregas during a 2010 World Cup quarter final match.

Numbers Game

Ronaldo is the all-time leading World Cup goalscorer with 15 goals. His country, Brazil has scored the most times, 210, followed by Germany with 206.

Shocks and controversy

All World Cups have their shock results and moments of drama, good and bad. Poor discipline, moments of madness and mistakes by officials also occur and are seen and discussed afterwards by millions.

Referees under pressure

For neutral viewers, shock results like world champions France being beaten by Senegal at the 2002 World Cup or Northern Ireland defeating Spain at the 1982 tournament help make the tournament more exciting. Referees try to get every decision correct but in fast, dynamic games, they are under great pressure and can make mistakes. At the 2006 World Cup, referee Graham Poll showed one player, Josip Simunic, three yellow cards when two is the maximum. During a game at the 2010 tournament between England and Germany, a shot from Frank Lampard clearly crossed the goal line but the goal wasn't given.

South Korea's Ahn Jung-Hwan turns in delight after scoring the goal that knocked Italy out of the 2002 World Cup and sent his team into the quarter finals.

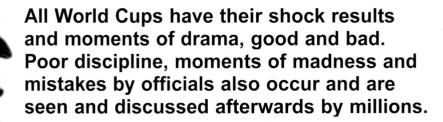

ON THE BALL

Peru's 1978 World Cup goalkeeper, Ramon Quiroga, often dribbled the ball out of his penalty area and was shown a yellow card for a foul on a Polish opponent in the other half of the pitch.

Seeing red

Peruvian midfielder Plácido Galindo was the first person to be sent off at a World Cup in 1930. Since that time a further 157 players have been told to leave the pitch by the referee. The fastest red card shown in a game was to Uruguay's José Batista who performed a bad foul tackle on Scotland's Gordon Strachan after just 56 seconds of their 1986 game. A team reduced to ten men by a red card are at a serious disadvantage but do not always lose. Marcel Desailly was sent off in the 1998 World Cup Final versus Brazil but the French team still triumphed 3-0. Desailly is one of five players to be sent off in a World Cup Final, the latest being the Netherlands' John Heitinga in 2010.

Numbers Game

Russian referee Valentin Ivanov showed a record **16** yellow cards to players in a single, bad-tempered 2006 match between Portugal and the Netherlands. **345** yellow cards were shown in total during that tournament.

Zinedine Zidane butts Italy's Marco Materazzi during the 2006 World Cup. Zidane was sent off and Italy won the game, but he was still made player of the tournament.

It's a knockout

Each team taking part in the World Cup plays three group games, with three points for a win and one for a draw. The top two points-scoring teams in a group qualify for the knockout phase of the competition called the 'Round of 16'. Quarter-finals and semi-finals follow before two sides reach the Final.

Early exits

Many fancied teams or former champions get knocked out early at the World Cup. In 2010, both the winners of the previous tournament, Italy, and the runners-up, France, finished bottom of their groups and were out of the World Cup, much to the shock and dismay of their fans. In Italy's group, New Zealand were the only team in the entire tournament to remain undefeated, but three points from three draws were not enough to propel them into the Round of 16. This was also the case for Switzerland who shocked Spain by beating them 1-0, but failed to get out of their group.

> *We feel like a small footballing nation and it hurts. There's nothing to say other than it's a catastrophe.*
>
> **Patrice Evra**, captain of the French team that made an early exit from the 2010 World Cup.

Róbert Vittek (left) celebrates after scoring one of the goals that helped Slovakia beat Italy 3-2 in Group F of the 2010 World Cup.

Knockout rounds

In a knockout round, each team plays a single game which it has to win to progress to the next round. Competition is fierce and teams including England, Portugal, Japan and the USA all exited the 2010 World Cup at the first knockout stage. If the game ends in a draw, extra time (two periods of 15 minutes) is played followed (if the scores are still level) by a nerve-shredding penalty shootout. Teams take five penalty kicks each to determine the winner and if the scores are tied, further kicks are taken, until one side misses and the other scores. Germany have the best record in World Cup penalty shootouts, winning all four they have contested (1982, 1986, 1990, 2006). England have the worst record, losing all three of their attempts (1990, 1998, 2006).

Ghana's Stephen Appiah puts the ball past Uruguay's goalkeeper, Fernando Muslera, to score during the penalty shootout that decided their 2010 World Cup quarter final game. Uruguay won the shootout 4-2.

The World Cup Final

The two winning semi-finalists have a few days off to prepare for the biggest game of their lives – a World Cup Final. Players' and fans' nerves jangle as the teams walk out on to the pitch. The biggest prize in world football is almost within their grasp.

Momentous match

The World Cup Final is played under the same rules as any major game. Of the more than 200 countries who have entered World Cup qualifying, only 12 have reached a World Cup Final and just eight have raised the trophy as winners.

Brazil are the only team to have scored five goals in the final, beating Sweden 5-2 in 1958 with two goals each from Vava and Pelé. These two players, along with Sir Geoff Hurst and Zinedine Zidane, have each scored three goals in one or more World Cup Finals.

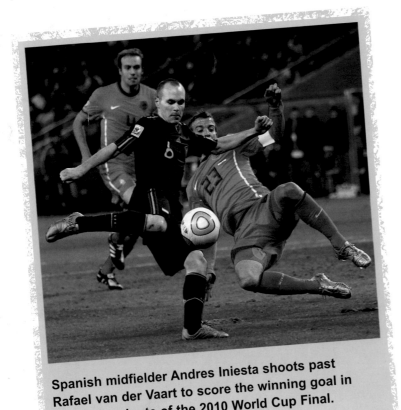

Spanish midfielder Andres Iniesta shoots past Rafael van der Vaart to score the winning goal in the 116th minute of the 2010 World Cup Final.

It's incredible. What a joy especially when you see how we won it. There aren't the words to describe what I am feeling. But the victory is the fruit of a lot of work.

Andres Iniesta
scorer of Spain's 2010 World Cup winning goal

Close contests

Two World Cup Finals have ended with the teams level after extra time and have gone to a penalty shootout. In 1994, Italian striker Roberto Baggio sent his penalty over the bar to give Brazil their fourth World Cup title. Italy again contested a penalty shootout in a final in 2006, playing against France. This time, they made no mistake, scoring all of their penalties to win their first World Cup since 1982. The 2010 World Cup Final looked like it, too, was heading for penalties before Spain scored with just four minutes of extra time to go.

Spain became the first European team to win a World Cup held on a different continent.

Numbers Game

WORLD CUP WINNERS

Brazil: 1958, 1962, 1970, 1994, 2002
Italy: 1934, 1938, 1982, 2006
Germany: 1954, 1974, 1990
Uruguay: 1930, 1950
Argentina: 1978, 1986
England: 1966
France: 1998
Spain: 2010

The play-off and awards

Other awards and achievements are decided in the days either side of the World Cup Final. First comes the play-off match to determine which of the two beaten semi-finalists will finish third. Then, at the end of each tournament, there's a range of awards that FIFA hands out to players and teams.

The battle for third place

Played in between the semi-finals and the World Cup Final, the third place play-off game is a tough challenge for teams. The players and fans are obviously disappointed at failing to reach the Final but have to regroup to play this game just days after tasting defeat. That said, recent play-off games have been entertaining matches with plenty of goals scored, from Sweden's 4-0 win over Bulgaria in 1994 to Germany scoring three goals to finish third in both the 2006 and 2010 World Cups.

In 2002, an entertaining 3-2 win by Turkey over South Korea saw the World Cup's fastest ever goal, a speedy strike after just 10.8 seconds by Turkey's Hakan Sükür.

Sammy Khedira scores Germany's third goal in their 3-2 win over Uruguay in the third place play-off in 2010. This entertaining match featured 34 shots at goal attempted by the two sides.

Awards and plaudits

The three most important individual player awards given by FIFA are the golden boot for the leading goalscorer, the golden ball for the best player of the tournament and the golden glove for the best keeper. Since 1970, FIFA also hand out a Fair Play award to the team with the best disciplinary record, meaning the fewest fouls, yellow and red cards. Brazil have won it four times and England twice (in 1990 and 1998 where they shared it jointly with France). An All-Star team is also picked each tournament. Only Franz Beckenbauer of Germany and Brazil's Djalma Santos have been named in All-Star teams at three different World Cups.

Numbers Game

AWARD WINNERS

2002
Golden Boot: Ronaldo
Golden Ball: Oliver Kahn
Golden Glove: Oliver Kahn

2006
Golden Boot: Miroslav Klose
Golden Ball: Zinedine Zidane
Golden Glove: Gianluigi Buffon

2010
Golden Boot: Thomas Müller
Golden Ball: Diego Forlan
Golden Glove: Iker Casillas

Germany's Thomas Müller (left), Diego Forlan of Uruguay (centre) and Spain's Iker Casillas (right) pose with the trophies awarded to them by FIFA after the 2010 World Cup.

2010 FIFA World Cup South Africa

The Women's World Cup

The FIFA Women's World Cup was first held in 1991 in China. Twelve teams took part in the competition, which was won by the United States. The tournament has been held every four years since, and was expanded to 16 teams for the 1999 World Cup and 24 teams for the 2015 World Cup, held in Canada.

Terrific tournaments

The Women's World Cup has helped promote the popularity of women's football, gaining large crowds and much media coverage. It follows a similar format to the male version with groups of four teams all playing each other once with the most successful teams in each group progressing to the Round of 16.

" No one expected much from our little team. But we prevailed game after game, and then we won. Our victory put women's football in Japan on the map.

Norio Sasaki
coach of Japan's 2011
winning women's team
"

At that stage the games become knockout, winner-takes-all matches leading to quarter-finals, semi-finals and a final. Each tournament has featured plenty of goals (87 in 2011 and 111 in 2007) and drama, with two finals going to penalty shootouts (1999 and 2011).

Japan's captain Homare Sawa looks to shoot after avoiding the tackle of USA midfielder, Carli Lloyd in the 2011 Women's World Cup Final. Sawa was voted the best player of the tournament and was also leading scorer with five goals.

Records and achievements

Two-time champions Germany hold the record for the biggest victory when they beat Argentina 11-0 at the 2007 tournament. One of their strikers, Birgit Prinz tops the all-time goalscoring table along with Brazilian attacker, Marta, both on 14 goals each. The USA's Abby Wambach is just one goal behind. The fastest World Cup goal was scored by Lena Videkull after just 30 seconds in Sweden's 1991 thrashing of Japan, 8-0. Twenty years later, the Japanese roared back to knock out the 2011 World Cup hosts, Germany, and favourites, USA in the final to become the first Asian side to win the World Cup.

Birgit Prinz holds the 2007 Women's World Cup trophy aloft. Unlike the men's competition, a different trophy is presented to and kept by the women's champions of each tournament.

Numbers Game

In the 1991 tournament Michelle Akers scored 10 goals in six games, the most by a player in any single tournament. Fellow US player Kristine Lilly has played in the most World Cup games, having notched up 30 matches.

27

Legends and records

The World Cup has been graced by some of the world's most outstanding footballers from brilliant attackers such as Johan Cruyff and Zinedine Zidane to great goalkeepers including Dino Zoff, Lev Yashin and Oliver Kahn.

World Cup legends

In defence, players such as England's Bobby Moore and Germany's Franz Beckenbauer were incredibly skilled readers of the game, able to time tackles with perfect precision. Another German great, Lothar Mattheus, played in defence and midfield. He notched up 25 matches at five different World Cups, the most of any player. In attack, Pelé holds many records, including being the only three-time winner of the World Cup and the youngest goalscorer. Argentina's Diego Maradona captained his side 16 times at a World Cup – more than any other player.

ON THE BALL

The youngest player at a World Cup was Norman Whiteside who was just 17 years and 42 days old when he played for Northern Ireland at the 1982 tournament.

Pelé mesmerises defenders with his incredible skills at the 1966 World Cup.

Goalscoring feats

The first World Cup hat-trick was scored by US striker Bert Patenaude against Paraguay in the 1930 World Cup. Forty-seven more have followed before the 2014 World Cup, the fastest taking less than eight minutes by Hungarian attacker, Laszlo Kiss at the 1982 World Cup. Gabriel Batistuta remains the only player to have scored hat-tricks at two different tournaments (1994, 1998) whilst Pelé remains the youngest hat-trick scorer – just 17 years old in 1958. One player went two goals better. At the 1994 World Cup, Russia's Oleg Salenko struck five times against Cameroon whose own striker, 42-year-old Roger Milla, was the oldest player ever to play at a World Cup.

Diego was capable of things no one else could match. The things I could do with a football, he could do with an orange.

Michel Platini, talking about Maradona at the 1986 World Cup

At the 1986 tournament, Diego Maradona scored what is regarded as the World Cup's greatest goal. He dribbled and weaved his way from inside his own half past most of the England team to score and put Argentina into the lead.

What it takes to be...

A World Cup star

Iker Casillas

Born in 1981, Casillas has been at Real Madrid all of his career and made his international debut for Spain at the age of 19. Desperate to be the best, he trained hard and took advice from more experienced goalkeepers and coaches to make improvements to his game. He is known for his strong powers of concentration, bravery and shot-stopping skills.

Career path

Casillas uses both hands to punch the ball firmly away to safety.

⚽ 2000: Youngest player to play in a Champions League final at the age of 19 years, 4 days as Real Madrid defeated Valencia 3–0.

⚽ 2002: In Spain's World Cup squad when injury to senior keeper, Santiago Canizares, saw him start his first World Cup games in goal. Responded with a string of great saves including saving two penalties.

⚽ 2006: Spain's first-choice goalkeeper for the World Cup, only conceding one goal in the group games.

⚽ 2010: Captained his national team in South Africa where his faultless goalkeeping helped Spain win their first ever World Cup. Named goalkeeper of the tournament.

⚽ 2012: Captained Spain to its second European Championships triumph in a row. Also became the first player to play in 100 international wins for his country.

Glossary

clean sheet when a team does not let in a goal during a whole game.

extra time a period of further play, usually two mini halves of 15 minutes each, played if the scores are level after 90 minutes.

foul unfair play such as pushing, tripping or pulling the shirt of an opponent. A referee who sees a foul will tend to stop play and give a free kick to the team that was being fouled.

friendly a football match not played as any part of a competition. Friendlies are played, for example, a few weeks before the World Cup, to give teams some match time before the tournament.

hat-trick three goals in a game.

host nation the nation or pair of nations in which a World Cup tournament is held.

FIFA *Fédération Internationale de Football Association,* the body that runs world football including the World Cup.

kick-off starting or restarting a game of football by kicking the ball forward from the centre spot marked on the pitch. A kick-off is used to start each half of a match. It is also used to restart the game after a goal has been scored.

penalty shootout a way used to decide a drawn game, with teams taking a series of penalty kicks.

Books

Record Busters: World Cup Football by Clive Gifford, Wayland 2014
World Cup Expert: Players by Pete May, Franklin Watts, 2013
World Cup Expert: Teams by Pete May, Franklin Watts, 2013
Football Focus: Teamwork and Tactics by Clive Gifford, Wayland, 2012
Inside Sport: World Cup Football by Clive Gifford, Wayland, 2010

Websites

www.fifa.com/worldcup/index.html
The official FIFA World Cup website is packed with features and news of qualifying games and tournaments.

www.fifa.com/womensworldcup/index.html
All about past and future Women's World Cup tournaments, with photos and videos.

www.planetworldcup.com/
A great website with details and stories about previous World Cups.

www.worldcup-soccer.info/
A treasure trove of facts and stats about each World Cup and the players and teams that took part.

Index

Football Focus

Contents of all titles in the series:

WAYLAND
www.waylandbooks.co.uk